The TV set arrives, 1953

INTRODUCTION

After ten years of austerity, the early 1950s saw rationing draw to an end. Restrictions on petrol, paper and soap all ended in 1950, and the green light was on for the launch of Eagle comic and Tide. Sweet rationing ended in time for Queen Elizabeth's Coronation, 1953, and Mount Everest was conquered a few days earlier. All seemed set for British recovery in a spirit of optimism. In many ways the Festival of Britain in 1951 had been the catalyst — a launch pad for new design and technical achievement — and yet life in Britain for most was still a struggle.

By the mid 1950s, the latest gadgets and home appliances were becoming affordable. Everyone aspired to model their homes on a G Plan "look", the radical textile design, the Dansette record player and, in the kitchen, the food mixer, electric fridge and hygenic Formica surfaces, plus the lightweight plastic cleaning brushes and pails. Housewives wanted to colour co-ordinate their rooms, so manufacturers provided fridges, soaps and toilet rolls in a range of colours — even Sifta Salt packs came in six colours. The teasmaid was seen as the ultimate in luxury living.

American culture was having an increasing effect on British life. Marilyn Monroe and Elvis Presley got people pulsating in different ways — the new beat of rock'n'roll swung to the fore when Bill Haley came to Britain in 1957. The Teddy Boys, with their hair brushed into quiffs (sculptured with the aid of Brylcreem) were perhaps manifesting the same rebellious spirit as James Dean in the USA, from where such films as Peyton Place (1957) had begun to undermine the fabric of society.

Bill Haley on tour, 1957

The novelty of the self-service supermarket began to change shopping habits, and the variety of groceries gave a new sense of excitement to shopping. Frozen foods were alluring — expensive, but "so convenient!". Sugar coated cereals provided a whole new taste sensation. Smokers were offered the innovations of filter tip and King Size cigarettes.

Pervading all else during the 1950s was the coming of television. Whereas children had to be coaxed to read through the Janet and John books, television instantly attracted little minds with Whirligig and Crackerjack and a host of animated characters. For adults the more serious side of life could be debated through Panorama or Tonight. Whatever else, TV was here to stay. In 1955 a fresh dimension was added (and a new language of slogans and jingles) when TV commercials appeared on the new independent channel.

Mills King Size launched, 1953

Fashion flourished, with an increasing emphasis on feminity, which may indeed have needed the Playtex or Silhouette corset to achieve the nipped-in waist to set off the voluminous cotton skirts.

Women were now establishing a new independence. Relieved of much of the drudgery and in a changing society, it was time for men to do the washing up or look after the baby. It was little wonder that Harold Macmillan could say with confidence by the end of the '50s that 'Britain had never had it so good!'

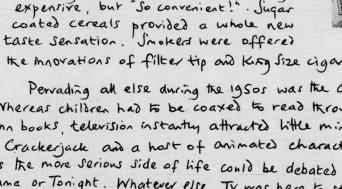

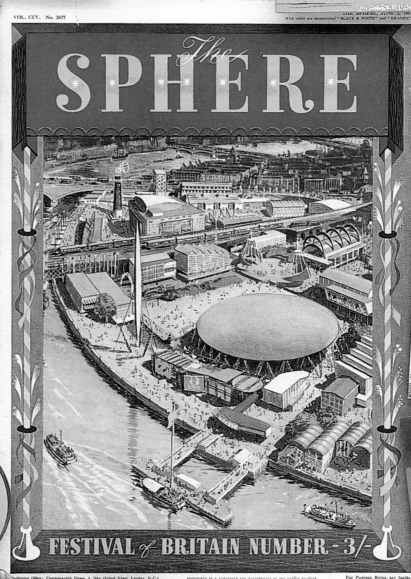

The aspirations of a generation: the Dansette record player, the television set (one with mauve tinted screen – a vague attempt at a colour image) and a choice of radios, including the new 'transistor' radio. The latest kitchen accessory was the Kenwood food mixer, launched at the Ideal Home Exhibition of 1950. The bright textiles livened up any home – curtains, cushions or aprons, and the baby feeding apron showed dad in action. Everything sparkled from the Phoenix and Pyrex dishes down to the harlequin lino, where the magazines and gramophone records were kept in order by the racks.

2. "Laundercentre" The first launderette had been opened in 1949 by Bendix using their washing machines; during the 1950s the idea caught on so that by the end of the decade there were about 2,000 launderettes around the country.

Centred on London's South Bank, the Festival of Britain in 1951 was nevertheless a national event. Abram Games' distinctive logo adorned the promotional posters, leaflets, souvenir compacts, embossed soap and Nestlé's chocolate bars. While the Dome of Discovery and the Skylon served as symbolic icons of the future, it was the Royal festival Hall which became the permanent legacy.

6. June 1953 saw the Coronation of Queen Elizabeth II. Sweet rationing had just ended and many families bought their first television set to watch the procession. Every type of souvenir was there - paper bags, bread wrappers and a cut-out coach on the Shredded Wheat box.

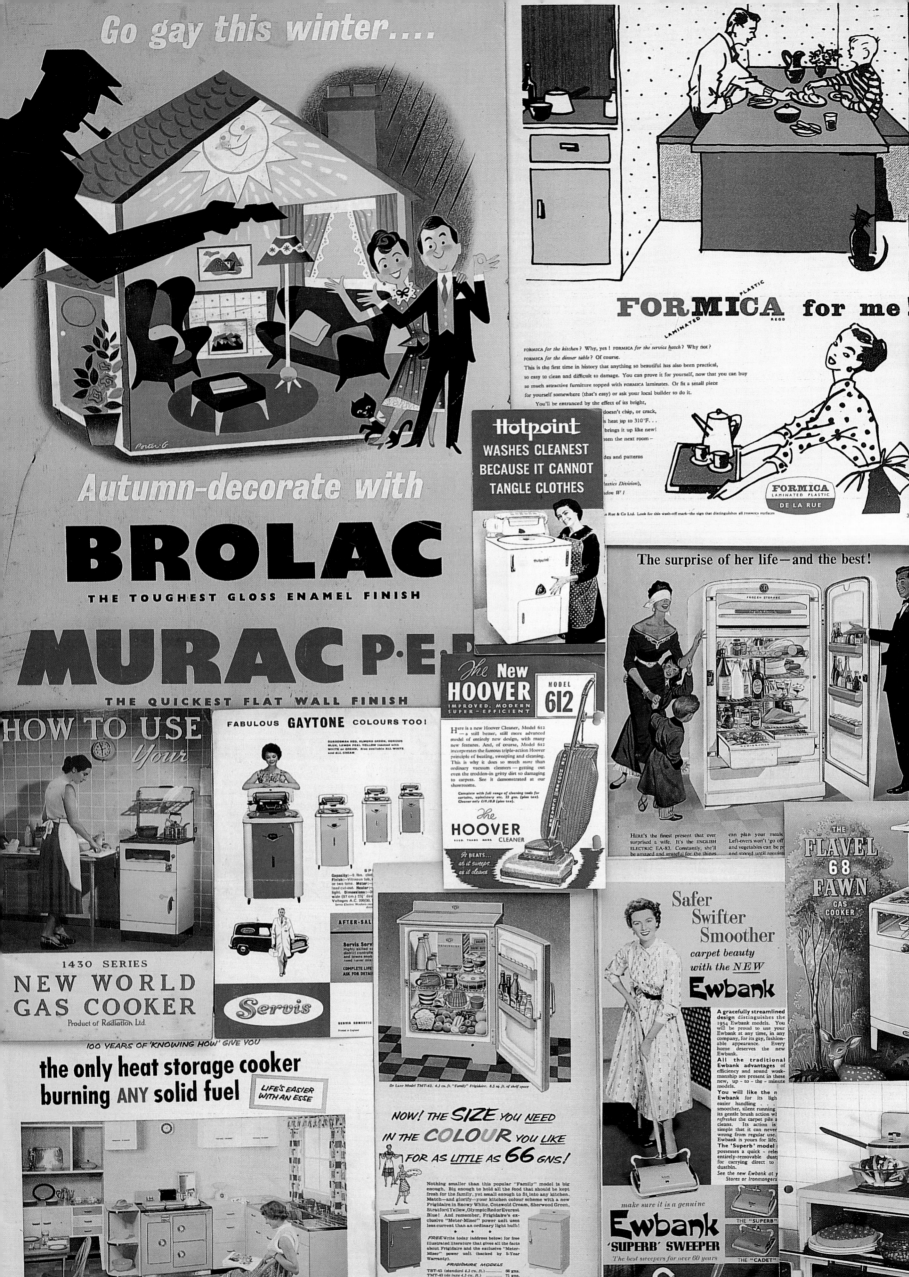

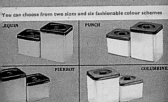

Happy faces in the home. Why? Because it all seemed to be easy, bright and clean. And because everything came in a range of colours — the Frigidaire, the Ewbank, the 'gaytone' colours of the Servis washer. The new types of plastic added their own gaiety to the kitchen scene: Alkathene was light and bright, Addis brushes made brighter work of household chores, Worcester Ware had its six fashionable colour schemes, and Tupperware was just about to have a party.

On previous pages 8 and 9

Radical new patterns abounded for kitchen fabrics and household crockery. The designs were often created years before they were commercially printed — it took time for manufacturers to risk production of styles the public were slow to appreciate.

The fabric 'Nautilus' by Mary Warren (bottom left) produced in 1955 and 'Hourglass' by W. Hertzberger (middle top) in 1956. For the plates, Terence Conran (Chequers), Hugh Casson (Cannes), Enid Seeney (Homemaker: created in 1955 but not available till 1958 exclusively from Woolworths) and Harold Bennett (Fantasia: bottom right).

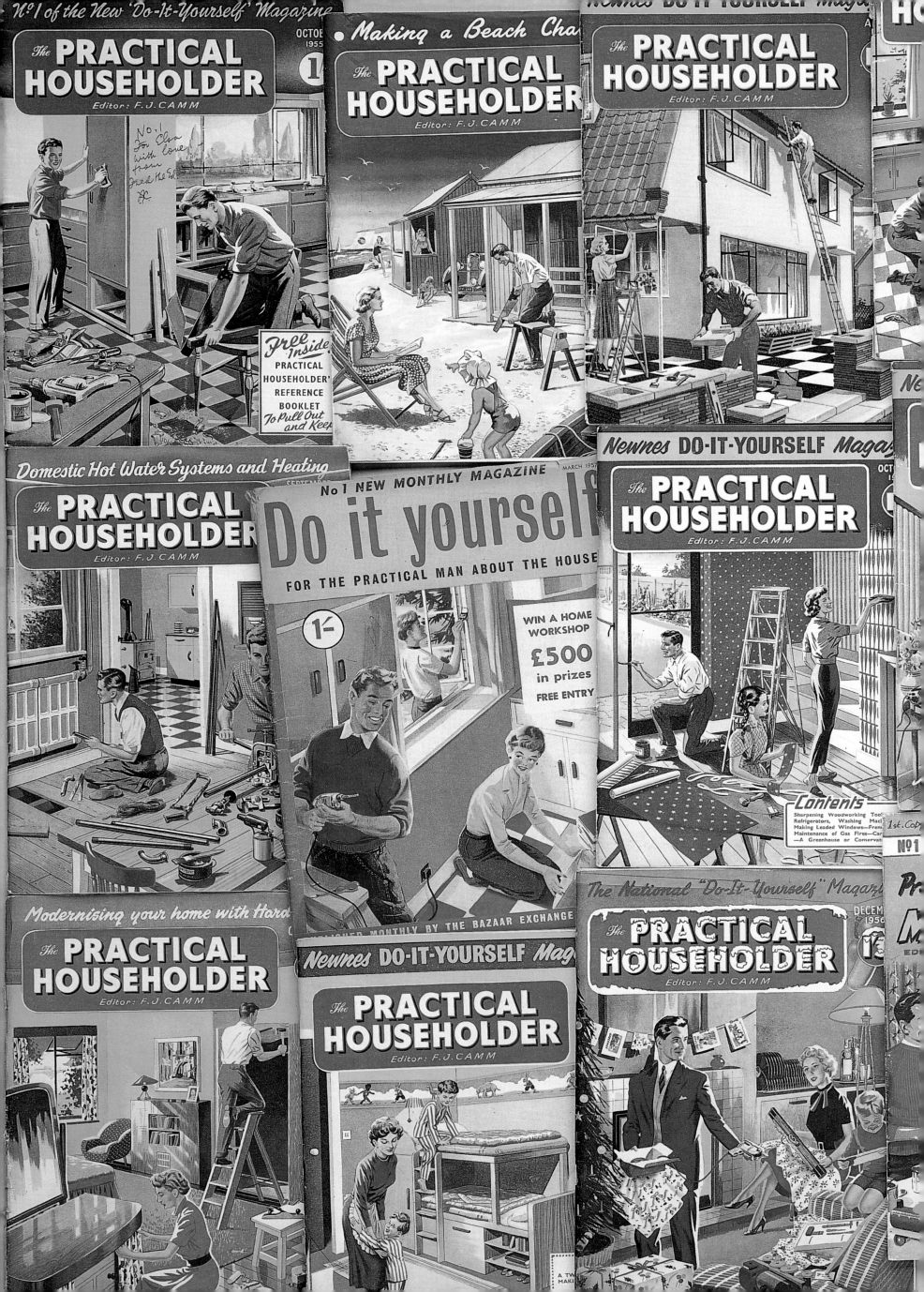

SEHOLDER
Editor: F.J.CAMM

AUGUST 1958

The **PRACTICAL HOUSEHOLDER**
Editor: F.J.CAMM

1'3

Landscape Gardening

Homemaker
THE PRACTICAL HOW-TO-DO-IT MONTHLY

Packed with **NEW** ideas for better homemaking
FREE inside!
Homemaker
COLOUR SCHEMER

N° 1
MARCH 1959
1'3

DO-IT-YOURSELF *Magazine*

MAY 1958

PRACTICAL HOUSEHOLDER
Editor: F.J.CAMM

1'3

FITTING SIMPLE SLIDING DOORS

Do it yours

FOR THE PRACTICAL MAN ABOUT THE

nising Staircase

Sept 1957

For Elsa (James to you) from Fred the Ed alias J.Camm

EW MAGAZINE FOR PLEASURE AND PROFIT.

cal **HOME NEY MAKER**
.J.CAMM

1'3

OCTOBER 1957

DAILY MAIL BOOK OF
HOUSE PLANS
1956

Yewnes **DO-IT-YOURSELF** *Magazine*

JUNE 1958

The **PRACTICAL HOUSEHOLDER**
Editor: F.J.CAMM

1'3

2'6

NEW DESIGNS—INCLUDING EXHIBITS AT THE
DAILY MAIL IDEAL HOME EXHIBITION 1956

Making a Refrigerator Sink Unit

By the mid 1950s the 'Do-it-yourself' passion had reached such proportions that a journal entirely devoted to DIY could be justified. The present for a man at Christmas was a Black & Decker or Wolf power drill, yet the phenomena of DIY was seemingly for all the family. For those with extra energy, Practical Home Money Maker was launched in 1957 — readers learnt how to "augment their income by means of practical & pleasurable hobbies" 13.

With the coming of the self-service store during the 1950s, packaging design had to adapt, becoming brighter and bolder to attract attention. Between 1949 and 1952 Tate & Lyle sugar packs fought off nationalisation with Mr Cube. Stork margarine

returned in 1954, but new arrivals were Kellogg's Frosted Flakes (1954), Quaker's Sugar Puffs (1954), Shreddies (1953, but renamed Cubs in 1958 when a new 'Shreddies' cereal was launched), Maxwell House instant coffee (1954), Nesquick (1955) and Jif Lemon (1956).

THE NEW

'ENGLISH ELECTRIC'
refrigerator

much more storage space

minimum kitchen space

large frozen food locker

easy de-frosting

easy cleaning

clear-view vegetable containers

thermostatic temperature cont[rol]

snap-release ice cubes

clear-view meat keepe[r]

adjustable shelves

standing room for quart bottle[s]

silent-running economy unit

Full of Fresh ideas!

BRINGING YOU   BETTER LIVING

The refridgerator was fast becoming a necessity for the home and yet by 1955 only 30% of homes owned one.
Retailers displayed the latest fridges invitingly full of produce - but it was all dummy packs or moulded rubber meat.
Manufacturers included Prestcold, Electrolux, Astral, Coldrator (promoted by the Archers), English Electric and Frigidare.

16.

As ownership of refridgerators grew gradually, so did the range of frozen foods. Although Smedleys had experimented with frozen foods in a few outlets towards the end of the 1930s, it was not until about 1950 that Birds Eye started to activate the market once more.

Birds Eye fish fingers arrived in 1955, followed by other manufacturers like Smedleys who had called them 'fish sticks' to begin with, changing them to 'fingers' as this seemed the more popular.

17.

After years of sweet rationing, it was little wonder that the nation's spirits were raised when restrictions were lifted in February 1953. Whilst Polo Mints and Spangles had been launched in 1948, further lines were added throughout the 1950s. Bounty had arrived tentatively in 1951 and Wagon Wheels (3¼" wide) in 1954. But most brands waited till the end of the decade, such as Week-End (1957), Munchies (1957), Galaxy (1958), Picnic (1958), Opal Fruits (1959) and Caramac (1959).

Improvements around the home with more advanced electrical appliances were reflected by improvements and innovations in household products. Washing machines were becoming more efficient and so were the washing powders, with an increasing range of detergents – Fab had arrived from America in 1949 ("Fabulous washing discovery. Up to 50% more economical than soap! It's all you need for all your needs!"), followed by Tide in 1950 ("for the clean, clean, cleanest weekly wash of all!"), Surf was launched in 1952, Daz the following year, and then in 1954 came the relaunch of Omo ("adds brightness to whites and coloureds too!"), Cheer in 1956 with a free duster in every pack, and Fairy Snow in 1957. Help was at hand with the washing-up – Quix had been around since 1948 with its special formula of concentrated suds, but it was not till the end of the '50s that washing-up liquids made an impact with brands like Squezy in 1956 ("one squeeze for each washing-up") and Lux Liquid launched in 1958 in a tin ("two shakes are all you need").

For furniture and floor polishes the new magic ingredient was silicone; another type of magic was the aerosol, taking tentative steps as, for instance, a fly spray and an air freshner. From 1949 a new type of foaming cleanser "polishes as it cleans" had arrived from the USA to compete with the traditional scouring powders like Vim, although it was the Ideal Home Cleanser with palm and olive soap that made the visual impact. In 1958 housewives had the benefits of two new products, "cleans at a touch" Flash powder for linoleum etc and Handy Andy in a bottle "cleans all your paintwork with a wipe"; for the handy man there was the new discovery of Polyfilla (also 1958) with its amazing positive bond. Improvements too were being made in toilet rolls where for years the needs of softness were at last being met by Andrex ("for those with delicate skin") and other brands. In an age of colour co-ordination it was not surprising that a range of colours extended to the toilet roll, as Velvet's Hermes proudly announced "now available in colours".

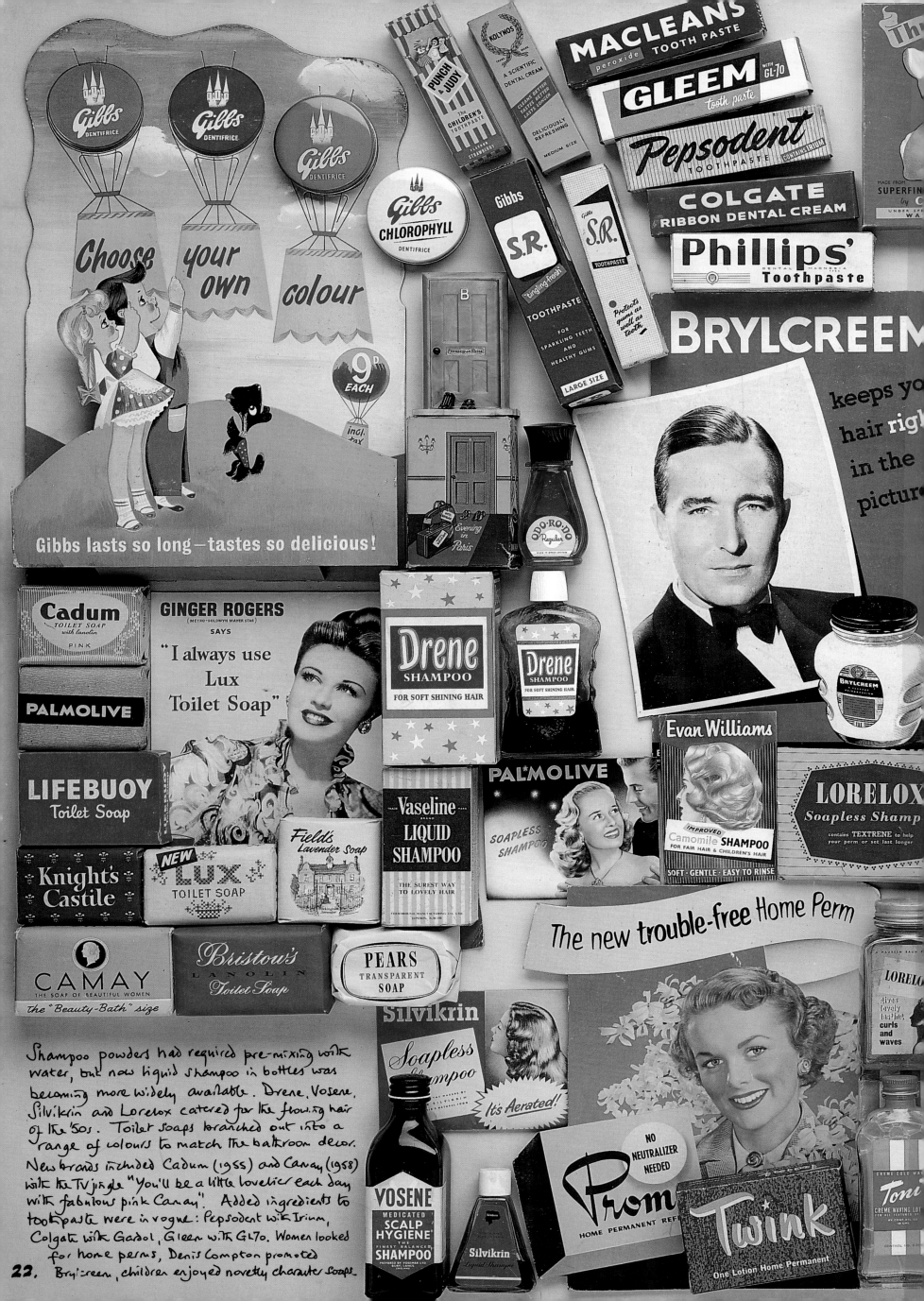

Choose your own colour

Gibbs lasts so long—tastes so delicious!

9ᴰ EACH incl. tax

GINGER ROGERS (METRO-GOLDWYN-MAYER STAR) SAYS "I always use Lux Toilet Soap"

Cadum TOILET SOAP with lanolin PINK

PALMOLIVE

LIFEBUOY Toilet Soap

Knight's Castle

NEW LUX TOILET SOAP

Field's Lavender Soap

CAMAY THE SOAP OF BEAUTIFUL WOMEN the "Beauty-Bath" size

Bristow's LANOLIN Toilet Soap

PEARS TRANSPARENT SOAP

Drene SHAMPOO FOR SOFT SHINING HAIR

Drene SHAMPOO FOR SOFT SHINING HAIR

Vaseline LIQUID SHAMPOO THE SUREST WAY TO LOVELY HAIR

PAL'MOLIVE SOAPLESS SHAMPOO

Evan Williams IMPROVED Camomile SHAMPOO FOR FAIR HAIR & CHILDREN'S HAIR SOFT · GENTLE · EASY TO RINSE

LORELOX Soapless Shampoo contains TEXTRENE to help your perm or set last longer

The new trouble-free Home Perm

Silvikrin

Soapless Shampoo It's Aerated!

NO NEUTRALIZER NEEDED

Prom HOME PERMANENT

Twink One Lotion Home Permanent

VOSENE MEDICATED SCALP HYGIENE THE FINEST BALANCED SHAMPOO PREPARED BY VOSENE MFG LTD

Silvikrin Liquid Shampoo

LORELO gives lovely lasting curls and waves

Toni CREME WAVING LOT

PUNCH & JUDY The CHILDREN'S TOOTHPASTE

KOLYNOS A SCIENTIFIC DENTAL CREAM

Gibbs CHLOROPHYLL DENTIFRICE

Gibbs S.R.

Gibbs S.R. TOOTHPASTE

ODO-RO-NO Regular

Evening in Paris

MACLEANS peroxide TOOTH PASTE

GLEEM with GL-70 tooth paste

Pepsodent TOOTHPASTE

COLGATE RIBBON DENTAL CREAM

Phillips' Toothpaste

BRYLCREEM keeps your hair right in the picture

BRYLCREEM

Shampoo powders had required pre-mixing with water, but now liquid shampoo in bottles was becoming more widely available. Drene, Vosene, Silvikrin and Lorelox catered for the flowing hair of the '50s. Toilet soaps branched out into a range of colours to match the bathroom decor. New brands included Cadum (1955) and Camay (1958) with the TV jingle "You'll be a little lovelier each day with fabulous pink Camay". Added ingredients to toothpaste were in vogue: Pepsodent with Irium, Colgate with Gardol, Gleem with GL70. Women looked for home perms, Denis Compton promoted Brylcreem, children enjoyed novelty character soaps.

MORLEY

Nylons

A **MURGATROYD** Product

Created by *Cantille Hosiery*

Week end

WITH
NON RUN
LADDER STOPS
AT TOP AND TOE

Enkalon

You'll feel like going places in
'**OHIO**'
15 denier
Needle point non-run
by
BEAR BRAND

Will-o'-the-Wisp
BY MINSTER

FASHIONED NYLONS

Twinco
SUN
GLASSES
1/9

NS AND 1/3
EEDLES
BRIGHT IDEAS FOR FAMILY & HOME
CROCHET · EMBROIDERY · DRESSMAKING
20 GIFTS NOVELTIES & TOYS

As the decade progressed, fashion moved from a
"flattering style in Herringbone" to the "ever-
popular pleated skirt in Terylene and wool".
Using man-made fibres the language of fashion
became one of brushed rayon gaberdine, nylon
lace, synthetic leather, Tricel pencil-slim skirts,
Winceyette night gowns and baby doll pyjamas.
Selling features included such words as minimum-
iron and drip-dry. Shoes ranged from the 3¼ inch
stiletto to the leather or suede bootee.
Mail order catalogues flourished with
"pay-as-you wear" plans.

TWELVE-PAGE KITCHEN BOOK INSIDE

GOOD HOUSEKEEPING

4½D

Nº1 GREAT *New* COLOUR WEEKLY FOR WOMEN

WOMAN'S DAY
5D EVERY TUESDAY
VOL.1 NO.1 · WEEK ENDING MARCH 22nd, 1958

HOUSE
wife
APRIL 1957 1/9

24 COLOUR SCHEMES
A forecast of the new fabrics, wallpapers and carpets

VICTOR BORGE
TV's funniest man

'I DRESS THE WORLD'S RICHEST WOMEN'

AUGUST 1955
MAN AND HOME
AND GOOD NEEDLEWORK MAGAZINE

ORY by LUCILLA ANDREWS

PICTURE
POST
MONDAY 4 MARCH 1957

CATTLE
TRAFFIC
The
truth

Vanity Fair
JULY 1956
16

For the Younger Smarter Woman

HOUSE
wife
AUGUST 1954 1/9
HOW TO HELP YOUR
HUS
PHYLLIS

SPECIAL HOLIDAY NUMBER
STORIES FOR DECKCHAIR READING BY L.A.G. STRONG AND DOROTHY WHIPPLE
SANDWICHES AND OPEN-AIR MEALS
GAMES FOR CAR AND BEACH

WOMAN'S
REALM
4D EVERY TUESDAY
Week ending February 22, 1958

No.1

EXTRA
8 page pull-out booklet of NEW knitting patterns

...icks for You! see page 24

A good variety of women's magazines were ready to discuss the issues of the day, such as Teenagery (the time when daughters start "playing about with boys") and A Man's Place in the Home — "what a husband will and won't do about the house, or should!" New arrivals at the newsagents in 1958 were Woman's Day (cookery recipes from Marguerite Patten and DIY advice from Peter Head) and Woman's Realm ("every woman finds happiness and fulfilment, as well as duty. This need never be a narrow domain, bounded though it is by kitchen, nursery and household chores. Indeed it can be the widest and most wonderful and most rewarding realm in the world").

27.

Whatever the pleasure Player's complete it

Player's Please

Filter tipped cigarettes started to establish their share of the market during the 1950s (although by 1955 they had less than 2% of sales). While Du Maurier had been around since 1929, new tipped brands were coming out like Bachelor (1950), Bristol (1955) and Olivier (1956). Tipped cigarettes were cheaper as they used less tobacco and enabled the smoker to economise, although there was some awareness that filters were better for the health. Another market being established was for a longer cigarette with brands like Rothmans King Size (1957), Churchmans K (1958) and Kingsway (1959), but these were not as long as the novelty cigarette, Joy Stick (five inches).

It was in 1959 that the swan on the Swan Vestas box finally started to swim the other way.

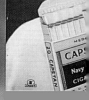

LION FIREWORKS

BROCK'S FIREWORKS

BROCK'S DISPLAY BOXES

DISPLAY OF 'CRYSTAL PALACE' BROCK'S FIREWORKS

HEMEL HEMPSTEAD · HERTS · ENGLAND

BROCK'S THE WORLD'S BEST

5'-
10'-
20'-
AND UPWARDS

HEMEL HEMPSTEAD HERTS. ENG.

All the fun of fireworks and bonfire on Guy Fawkes
night, the 5th November — the anticipation of the
fizz and whizz, the big bangs or the whoosh of
rockets. Wise guys bought the names that sounded
best: Witches Caldron, Floral Spray, Mighty Atom,
Satellite Rocket, Mighty Crash, Silver Rain, Dragon Flame.

31

A diversity of reading for children, to cater for all ages. Youngsters had Muffin's ABC book, Noddy stories from Enid Blyton and the Reverend Awdry's tales of Thomas the Tank Engine or Percy the Small Engine.

Teenagers could rely on the cowboy adventures of Roy Rogers and Gene Autry, the thrills of James Bond in Dr No or the mischievous behaviour of the Larkins in the Darling Buds of May.

For many children (and adults) their world went into outer space with science fiction where Rick Random takes on the space pirates, "with racing finger Rick opened the tiny radio....."

33.

The ending of paper rationing in 1950 cleared the way for a new wave of comics. Quick off the mark was Eagle, launched in April 1950. Eagle was the creation of the Reverend Marcus Morris who had wanted to provide boys with better reading material than the imported crime comics from America. On the cover began the adventures of Dan Dare, Pilot of the Future, drawn by Frank Hampson. For girls, School Friend was published in May 1950, followed by Girl in 1951, the companion comic to Eagle. Bunty arrived in 1958.

The growth of television inspired TV Comic (1951) and TV Fun (1953), while for the youngsters came Robin (1953) Swift, Jack & Jill and Playhour (all 1954), Zip (1958) and Harold Hare's Own Paper (1959). Other notable comics were Topper (1953), Tiger (1954) with Roy of the Rovers and Beezer (1956). An attempt to compete with Eagle was made by Rocket launched in 1956 and edited by Douglas Bader, the WWII pilot ace, but it only lasted 32 missions.

The inherent interest in outer space plus the popularity of Eagle's Dan Dare ensured a huge demand for Dan Dare and space related toys. Walkie-Talkie sets particularly popular along with a host of guns with appropriate abilities, such as high frequency resonator or rockets with secret message chamber (the word "safety" was added to calm worried parents). Dan Dare toothpowder was issued by Calverts along with a picture card album, and Lifebuoy Soap supplied the Dan Dare Interplanetary Stamp Folder, plus stamps.

Previous pages 38-39
Traditional toys and games like building sets, dolls, trains (electric as well as clockwork) and Post Office sets were now joined by popular toys of the 50s + Magic Robot (always gives the right answer) remote control Driving Test, Mr Potato Head and the frustrating Tap-Tap toy with hammer and nails. Cowboy guns had been a feature of children's toys for many years; the Cisco Kid hit town in 1954 on the TV screen.

In the late 1940s hundreds of businesses were set up, some making toys and games. Many failed, but the creator of Subbuteo survived; originating in 1947, the box on page 39 dates from 1958. The origins of Airfix date back to 1939 when Nicholas Kove started to manufacture cheap rubber toys. By 1948, with his main business making plastic combs in decline, Kove was asked to produce a replica tractor for Fergusson. When some were later sold to the public in kit form, he saw the potential of the product. In 1952 Airfix launched the Golden Hind kit in a plastic bag, selling at 2/- in Woolworths. By 1958 kits were sold in boxes with striking illustrations, such as for the Wellington bomber.

This page
At the beginning of the 1950s, the leading name in diecast models was that of Dinky. However, in 1956 The Mettoy Company, which had been a toy producer since 1933, began to create its range of Corgi toys. Their vehicles were made to a uniform scale; the cars had plastic windows and they had more detail than those of Dinky models. In the following year a diecast chassis was added and in 1959 the vehicles ran more easily with the "glideamatic suspension".

40.

Next pages 42-43

Being up with the latest developments, Corgi produced miniature versions of the new missile technology, the year after it had been on display at the Farnborough Air Show of 1957 – here were the Thunderbird Guided Missile by English Electric and the Bristol Bloodhound.

Matchbox Toys were the creation of two ex-servicemen who had set up business in 1947. Following the success of a miniature coronation coach in 1953, the diecast Matchbox Toys were on sale at 1/6ᵈ each the following year.

All the fun of television game shows to play at home – "I'm in Charge" with Bruce Forsyth, "Take Your Pick" with Michael Miles and "Double Your Money" with Hughie Green. Popular television dramas like Emergency Ward 10, Dixon of Dock Green with Jack Warner and the Adventures of Robin Hood with Richard Green also had their toys. Comedy too had boxed games like for Hancock's Half Hour and Jimmy Edwards' Whacko. The Lone Ranger first appeared on the small screen in 1956.

Pelham Puppets had begun in 1949 – some of their puppets were of television characters such as Mr Turnip, who appeared with the comedian Humphrey Lestocq on the children's programme Whirligig (this TV favourite ran for five years and also featured the lively cowboy Hank; in 1955 Whirligig was replaced by Crackerjack hosted by Eamonn Andrews). Watch With Mother had begun in 1950 and its first star was Andy Pandy, followed in 1952 by the Flowerpot Men; Muffin the Mule had been around since 1946, while Sooty first appeared on TV in 1952 and Pinky and Perky came on the screen in 1957.

41.

BELL'S new hilarious, exciting, game

SGT BILKO

based on the popular **PHIL SILVERS** show

... can **YOU** beat bilko?

a family game for all ages

T. FRANK BALLINGER in

M Squad

BASED ON THE EXCITING T.V. SERIAL

A GAME OF MYSTERY AND SUSPENSE

THE ARMY GAME

LAUGHTER & FUN FOR ALL THE FAMILY

ANDY PANDY
JIC-SAW

MUFFIN THE **MULE** ON THE TOY TELEVISION SET

join **Robin Hood**

AND HIS MERRY MEN

in this thrill-packed game!

from the exciting ITV show starring *Richard Greene*

Another **CHAD VALLEY** T.V. Game

HANCOCK'S HALF HOUR

MADE IN ENGLAND

BY ARRANGEMENT WITH ALAN SIMPSON AND RAY GALTON

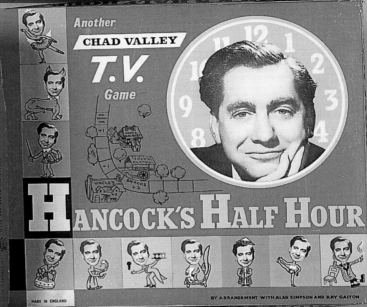

COOKERY OUTFIT
BY ARRANGEMENT WITH SOOTY CONCESSIONS LTD.   SERIAL No. 605

WITH SOOTY

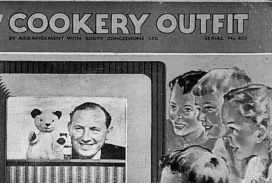

ZOO QUEST
BY ARRANGEMENT WITH THE B·B·C

HANK'S RANCH
Shooting Game

MUFFIN DERBY
RACE GAME

Palitoy

Peter Brough's

ARCHIE ANDREWS

Ventriloquial DOLL

YOU *Can do it!*

• EASY TO WORK • MOUTH OPENS AND
SHUTS • READY TO OPERATE • DURABLE
PLASTIC HEAD • HANDS • AND SHOES
For Boys and Girls 6 to 60 years!

GREEN

HIGHWAY PATROL

based on the ITV show for
BRODERICK
CRAWFORD

an exciting & competitive game for 2 to 4 p

Introducing **Muffin** JUNIO

WAGON TRAIN

ALL THE RIP-ROARING THRILLS OF THE WILD WEST!

An exciting game
for all ages

starring **WARD BOND**
and
ROBERT HORTON

based on I.T.V.'s most
popular western series

'LOWBOY' TV (Non-fringe)
An exquisite example of Pye Contemporary TV—specially designed for the home of to-day. Features 13-Channel Tuning, Automatic Picture Control, 17" Black Screen. Twin Speakers are incorporated in a specially built acoustic enclosure providing vivid, true-to-life sound. Available finished either in French Walnut or Japanese Sen, in a charming 'Lowboy' cabinet.

Model LB17NF   87 GNS. TAX PAID.

THE 'CONTINENTAL 21'
This new and brilliantly conceived Pye TV is designed to bring a touch of Continental magic to your living-room. Finished in Continental style in dark walnut veneers with contrasting brass metal trims—it features 13-Channel Tuning, Automatic Picture Control, a giant 21" Black Screen and Twin Loud-speakers. Available as a table model, or with matching legs.

Model CTM21   95 GNS. TAX PAID.

'CONTINENTAL 17'
...table TV styled in the gay, good-...manner. 13-Channel Tuning, ...Control and 17" Black Screen. ...a variable Tone Control give ...te realism. Finished in highly ...ers.

81 GNS. TAX PAID.

TELEVISION IN YOUR HOME
EVERYTHING THE POTENTIAL VIEWER NEEDS TO KNOW

TWO SHILLINGS NET

J-MAST THREE
Extreme discrimination

So many end up with BUSH

SENSATIONAL!
Remove eyestrain filter for colour viewing.
T.V. Hand Colour Viewer
SEE BLACK AND WHITE PICTURES IN COLOUR
Puppets and Cartoons in colour
See your Holiday Films in colour
See Black and White Photos in colour
See Black and White Comics in colour
A MUST FOR CHILDREN
Should you get fingermarks on Viewer polish lightly with soft cloth

Copyright

ONLY 7/6d.

4d EVERY WEDNESDAY

ALL SIZES   ALL SPEEDS
ALL YOURS FOR 14 GUINEAS

14 GNS. TAX PAID
...6 plus tax £3-11-6

High Fidelity by Currys

DECCALIAN

PHILIPS 'MAGIC BOX'

The CHAMPION THREE SPEED PORTABLE RECORD REPRODUCER

Dansette POPULAR

of Quality

The powerful Amplifier gives superior reproduction, latest ...BSR 4-speed A.C. main motor plays all size discs. Inde...pendent tone and volume controls. Dual turnover pick-up ...head, fitted with sapphire stylus for full tonal value from ...standard and long-playing records. Italian styled cabinet ...available in a variety of colours.

PRICE 11 GNS.
(Tax Paid)

Manufactured by Dansette Products Ltd., 112/116 Old Street, London, E.C.1.

HOME TRIALS
Sell PYE Hi Fi

MONEY

STOP INTERFERENCE

...get a clear picture with
Labgear
filters and suppressors

EKCO tele-gram
including V.H.F. radio and a 4-speed record player

model TCG316

THE POSTMASTER GENERAL APPEALS TO MOTORISTS
"SUPPRESS TELEVISION INTERFERENCE"

Unsuppressed motor vehicle ignition systems cause serious interference with television reception. These photographs show the devastating effect and the improvement when a suppressor is fitted.

BEFORE   AFTER

IS FASHIONS

The Coronation in 1953 added impetus to the sale of television sets – some 100,000 sets were sold in that year. In 1950 there had been just 700,000 viewers, and the first Eurovision link was forged with pictures coming direct from France. As the network extended to more parts of the country and commercial television came in 1955, so by 1957 there were over seven million regular viewers. The TV Hand Colour Viewer was one of many ways that people tried to get "wonderful multi-colour pictures".

For music enthusiasts the light weight vinyl record at 45 rpm was a boon and the gradual introduction of high-fidelity (Hi Fi) in the late 1940s enhanced the sound quality. Long-playing records at 33⅓ rpm had started in 1950, while stereophonic discs were released in 1958.

45.

RADIO TIMES
JOURNAL OF THE BBC   PRICE TWOPENCE

Radio Times [Incorporating World Radio]
July 21, 1950.   Vol. 108 – No. 1397
Registered at the G.P.O. as a Newspaper

PROGRAMMES FOR
JULY 23—29

VAUGHAN WILLIAMS
on 'Bach, the Great Bourgeois'
Friday in the Third Programme

BLIGH OF THE BOUNTY
Study of a controversial figure presented
in eight weekly episodes (Wednesday)

PROMENADE CONCERTS
Broadcasts throughout the week

HILAIRE BELLOC
A tribute for his eightieth birthday
by Desmond MacCarthy (Sunday, Home
Service; Thursday, Third Programme)

THE RISE OF A PARTY
Account of the events that led to the
formation of the Labour Party fifty
years ago (Tuesday)

FRED HOYLE
First of his eight lectures on The Nature
of the Universe (Wednesday)

HULLO THERE!
The summer holiday programme for
young people—Monday to Saturday

'DON GIOVANNI'
Opening performance of this year's
Salzburg Festival (Thursday)

RACING AT GOODWOOD
The Stakes on Wednesday and
The Cup on Thursday

P.C. 49

comes back on the beat in the Light
Programme on Thursday and you will
be able to follow his adventures week

The only paper giving **NEW TV** programmes in full   No. 1

TV TIMES
OFFICIAL PROGRAMMES   THURSDAY **SEPT 22**—SATURDAY

Every

	Page
Editorial and Viewing Guide......	3
Messages of welcome to the new TV......	4
Cover Story......	5
Stars in Pictures......	6-7

COVER PICTURE

PATRICIA DAINTON (left) plays
the part of Sally in "Sixpenny
Corner," the Monday-to-Friday mid-
morning serial.

LUCILLE BALL (right) appears in
the famous "I Love Lucy" to be seen
at 9 o'clock.

Sportscreen...
"I'm no Crooner"
by Guy Mitchell
Morning Magazine
Mary Hill introduces
'Young Viewers'
Looking Around...
Programme Previews

MIDLAND EDITION

Radio Times [Incorporating World Radio]   April 21, 1950
Vol. 107 - No. 1384.   Registered at the G.P.O. as a Newspaper

RADIO TIMES
JOURNAL OF THE BBC   PRICE TWOPENCE

PROGRAMMES FOR
APRIL 23—29

Woman's Hour Celebrates its 1,000th Edition on Friday

BBC SOUND AND TELEVISION
PROGRAMMES. SEPTEMBER 14—20

Radio Times [Incorporating World Radio]
September 12, 1952. Vol. 116, No. 1505
Registered at the G.P.O. as a Newspaper

RADIO TIMES
JOURNAL OF THE BBC   PRICE THREEPENCE

Archie Andrews Resumes His Education

September 24th, 1955   Vol. 5   No. 13

TV mirror
4ᴰ WEEKLY

N° 1 of the NEW WEEKLY
for Viewers and Listeners

★

In This Issue:

**THE FIRST OF TWO
FREE BOOKLETS:**
Radio and TV WHO'S WHO and QUIZ

★

**ACTING FOR VIEWERS
by SARAH CHURCHILL**

★

**MUST BE WON
360 gn. TV RADIOGRAM**

TERRY-THOMAS

TV mirror
4ᴰ

September 12th, 1953 Vol. 1 No. 3   Every Wednesday

Radio Times [Incorporating World Radio]   March 25, 1955
Vol. 126. No. 1637.   Registered at the G.P.O. as a Newspaper

WEST OF ENGLAND EDITION

RADIO T[IMES]
JOURNAL OF THE BBC

**The Grove Family
of Television**

It is just a year ago that the television cameras first
began recording the everyday happenings of the
Grove household. Another domestic episode will be
televised on Friday. To mark this first anniversary we

T[V]
[mirr]or
4ᴰ

Every

March 1[...]

TV
mirror

'TONIGHT'
RETURNS WITH
Cliff Michelmore

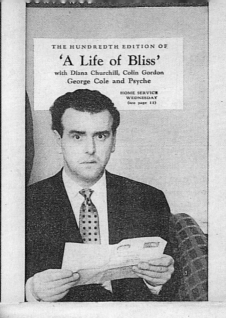

THE HUNDREDTH EDITION OF
'A Life of Bliss'
with Diana Churchill, Colin Gordon
George Cole and Psyche
HOME SERVICE
WEDNESDAY
(see page 11)

Richard Dimbleby
opens BBC Television's Window on the World
PANORAMA

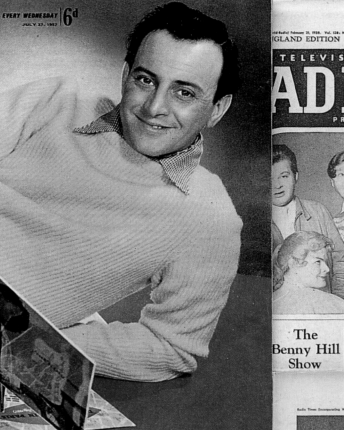

EVERY WEDNESDAY 6d
JULY 27, 1957

V
rror

4½d Every
Wednesday

▲ DAVID JACOBS REVIEWS THE LATEST RECORDS
PET CLARK: THE MEN IN MY LIFE
TAKE YOU INSIDE TV's NEW THEATRE

ENGLAND EDITION   FEBRUARY 23

TELEVISION BBC AND SOUND
RADIO TIMES
PRICE THREEPENCE

The
Benny Hill
Show

LONDON EDITION   No. 96
Sept 1—Sept 7 ITV Programmes Pages 20-33
TV TIMES

ROBIN DAY

AND TELEVISION

CH 27—APRIL 2

ES
THREEPENCE

A Giggle of Goons

JUNE 14—20

TELEVISION BBC AND SOUND
RADIO TIMES
PRICE FOURPENCE

Phil Silvers
The irrepressible Sergeant
Bilko in person is
Tommy Trinder's guest in
THE FIRST
TRINDER BOX
SATURDAY TELEVISION

Tommy Trinder
written on
page 3

WELSH EDITION   SEPTEMBER 20—26

TELEVISION BBC AND SOUND
RADIO TIMES
PRICE FOURPENCE

Back from
his 'hols'

TONY HANCOCK
has been on holiday

Radio and television
created many
household names:
· Brian Reece as PC49
· Tommy Cooper
· Lucile Ball
· Cliff Michelmore
· George Cole in
  'A Life of Bliss'
· Richard Dimbleby
· Archie Andrews & Brough
· David Attenborough
  with Zoo Quest
· David Jacobs with
  Juke Box Jury
· Benny Hill
· Robin Day
· Terry Thomas
· Frankie Howerd
· David Nixon,
  TV's magic man
· Eamonn Andrews
· The Goons of
  Peter Sellers,
  Spike Milligan &
  Harry Secombe
· Tony Hancock
· Phil Silvers
  as Bilko

The Archers were first broadcast in 1951,
celebrating 2000 editions by 1958. The death
of Grace Archer was broadcast on the day that
commercial TV began in 1955. BBC TV's
counterpart was the Grove family (named
after Lime Grove Studios); starting in 1954
they became 'a must' on Friday evenings.

47.

Elegant **new** SINGER *Gazelle*

NEW STANDARD Vanguard Estate Car

Vauxhall *Victor*

THE MOST EXCITING MOTORING NEWS FOR YEARS

AUSTIN A35 SALOON
AND FOUR-DOOR MODELS

ZODIAC

752 LME

IMPROVED PERFORMANCE · INCREASED SAFETY

Publication No. H & E 97—29

IT'S WIZARDRY ON WHEELS!

The Revolutionary
"QUALITY FIRST"
MORRIS *Mini-Minor*

re Miles Per Coupon!

APRIL 1957
1'3

Practical Motorist
& Motor Cyclist
R·MAINTENANCE·OVERHAUL
Editor: F.J. CAMM

SHELL

sheer joy of driving it

OH 898465 — OH 898465
Motor Fuel Ration Book
Registered No. of Vehicle
MOTOR
080170
NTH ONE
LG 080170
Motor Fuel Ration Book
MOTOR CAR
(inc. Tricycle)
not exceeding
1100
C.C.
1-9
H.P.

MF1672200
Motor Fuel Ration Period
FIRST
RATIONING PERIOD
Motor Car
10-13 H.P.
1 ONE
UNIT

SECOND MONTH
POD
785
2 UNITS

Cars in the early 1950s were influenced by the bulbous shapes and chrome features of American cars. The Morris Oxford of 1953 could boast of hydraulic brakes, steering column gear shift, four-speed synchromesh gearbox and self-cancelling trafficators.

Estate cars were becoming part of the motoring scene, like the Standard Ten Companion of 1955.

Following the Suez crisis, petrol rationing was introduced for a time between December 1956 and April 1957. Petrol prices were rising and smaller cars with better fuel consumption were required. Then in 1959 came the revolutionary Austin and Morris mini, costing around £500. A dream to handle, "She can nip in where the grocer's boy usually parks his bicycle!"

49.

For health and happiness ...

RIDE A **Royal Enfield**

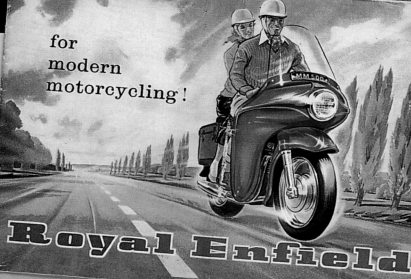

With petrol increases in the late 1950s, the motor cycle and scooter grew in popularity — they beat the traffic jams too. In 1959 Royal Enfield announced their 'Airflow' styled fairing, made from glass-fibre reinforced polyester resin — a 20% petrol saving.

50.

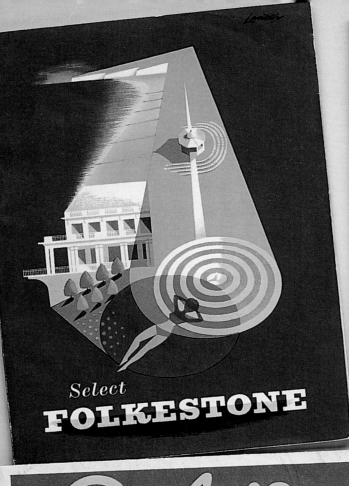

Select FOLKESTONE

WESTON SUPER-MARE

Blackpool
FOR HAPPY HEALTHY HOLIDAYS

Butlin's FOR YOUR HOLIDAY

where you make
new friends . . .

The **ISLE of MAN**
for Happy Holidays

The Art of **SURF-RIDING**
ON THE

BRITISH RAILW
**Holida
Guid
19**

SOUTH & SOUTH EAST
INCLUDING THE CHANNEL ISLANDS
1/-

HASTINGS AND ST. LEONARDS

Butlin's
where you make
new friends!

FREE
BROCHURE
SEE OVERLEAF

WHATEVER THE WEATHER, IT'S FINE AT Butlin's

Butlins for a REAL
Family
Holiday!

FREE
BOOKLET

BUTLIN'S—WHERE YOU MAKE

Butlin's-
for the
Time of your
Life!

FREE
BROCHURE
SEE OVERLEAF

Butlin's—WHERE YOU MAKE NEW FRIENDS

LOOK!
HERE'S YOUR
1955 HOLIDAY

PRESTATYN HOLIDAY CAMP

Holiday Haunt
1959
BY BRITISH RAILW

WEST OF ENGLAND
(SOMERSET DEVON & CORNWALL)
SOUTH & CENTRAL WALES

Beach balls and bikinis were the popular
image of seaside holidays on Britain's
beaches. The holiday camps were
having a boom time. Butlins had
six camps including one in Southern
Ireland. It was a carefree way of
family enjoyment – glamorous
grandmother or knobbly knees competitions.

52

Flight Information BCPA

British Commonwealth Pacific Airlines

Enjoy **luxury living** on your trip across the Pacific

Step aboard a BCPA DC-6 and luxury living becomes your normal routine! In the restful atmosphere of the "pressurised" and air-conditioned cabin, you relax in the deep-cushioned seats . . . enjoy delicious meals and snacks (there's a well-stocked bar, too) . . . discover the friendly yet courteous service of ever-attentive hostesses.

In addition, BCPA is the only Pacific airline which provides a full-length sleeper for **every** passenger — not just a converted seat, but a comfortable bed in a curtained compartment, complete with mattress, sheets, blankets . . . even a reading lamp. Remember, this **added** comfort costs you nothing extra with BCPA.

CLIPPER PORTFOLIO

PAN AMERICAN WORLD AIRWAYS
The System of the Flying Clippers

NEW YORK by CLIPPER

PAN AMERICAN WORLD AIRWAYS
THE WORLD'S MOST EXPERIENCED AIRLINE

B.C.P.A BRITISH COMMONWEALTH PACIFIC AIRLINES
THE "SOUTHERN CROSS" ROUTE
Printed in Australia

5/- 477841   0602 23 47459
Received the sum of five shillings against the
AIRPORT SERVICE CHARGE
PLEASE RETAIN AND SHOW ON DEMAND

BEA
Passenger ticket and baggage check

ISSUED BY
BRITISH EUROPEAN AIRWAYS

UNITED AIR LINES
THE "MAIN LINE" COAST-TO-COAST

BEA ROUTE MAP
For the UNITED KINGDOM
Channel Islands & Isle of Man

BEA route map
for the United Kingdom
Channel Islands and the Isle of Man

BRITISH EUROPEAN AIRWAYS

Introducing **BEA** ELIZABETHAN
BRITISH EUROPEAN AIRWAYS

Introducing **BEA** ELIZABETHAN
BRITISH EUROPEAN AIRWAYS

BEA takes you there and brings you back
BRITISH EUROPEAN AIRWAYS

YHA CONTINENTAL TRAVEL KEY
1953 PRICE 1/6

WITH GULLIVER... WITH *Confidence!*
1952 *Gulliver's Travels*

Your coach awaits
See the Continent via **Global**

holidays in ITALY 1955

THOS. COOK & SON LTD · DEAN & DAWSON LTD

For most, travel overseas was seen as an adventure, and although more people went by 'plane, the organised trip on a coach to Continental destinations was a popular alternative. In 1955 Global offered a 12 day grand coach tour to Paris, Brussels, Amsterdam, Berne and Bonn for 46 gns. or 14 days on five rivieras for 54 gns.

By 1959 the Spanish package holiday had begun – 15 days in Palma, Majorca from 44 gns. "its fascinating streets are jam-packed with shops and cafes, wine cellars and nightclubs. And right beside the gaiety of the town lie the pleasures of the beaches and the sea."

Even though there had been trials with jet airliners, like the De Havilland Comet, during the early 1950s, it was not until 1958 that commercial jet travel began.

STEVE

SCHOOLS
LIBRARY
SERVICE
RIFS

CLIFF
Sings

THE EVERLY BROTHERS - No. 5
PROBLEMS
LOVE OF MY LIFE
TAKE A MESSAGE TO MARY
POOR JENNY
A CADENCE Recording
RE-A 1229
LONDON
RECORDS

The
GIRL
"LOVE ME
PRES

HIS MASTER'S VOICE
45 r.p.m. EXTENDED PLAY

ROCK'N
ROLL
Razzle dazzle
Two hound dogs
Burn that candle
Rock-a-beatin'
boogie
BILL HALEY
AND HIS COMETS
45 R.P.M. EXTENDED PLAY RECORD
Brunswick
RECORDS
OE 9214

Brunswick
RECORDS
OE 9250

TWANGY

UP AND DOWN
LOST ISLAND
BERRY HILL
RE MY SUNSHINE
DUANE EDDY

PERRY COMO
"HIS MASTER'S VOICE" RECORDS

MAX

BYGRAVES

AS
I
LOVE
YOU
PHILIPS

Shirley
Bassey

Come fly
with me
FRANK SINATRA
with BILLY MAY and his orchestra
Capitol
HIGH FIDELITY

MORE THAN EVER
(COME PRIMA)
TED HEATH
ARE MARCH
DECCA
THE BLUES
THE ARMY GAME
THE BLUES
Ted Heath

top ten

DECCA GROUP No. 56

1	WEAR MY RING AROUND YOUR NECK	Elvis Presley RCA1058
2	A WONDERFUL TIME UP THERE/ IT'S TOO SOON TO KNOW	Pat Boone HLD8574
3	LOLLIPOP	The Chordettes HLD8584
4	KEWPIE DOLL	Perry Como RCA1055
5	CATCH A FALLING STAR/ MAGIC MOMENTS	Perry Como RCA1036
6	SWINGIN' SHEPHERD BLUES	Ted Heath F11000
7	TULIPS FROM AMSTERDAM/ YOU NEED HANDS	Max Bygraves F11004
8	PRINCESS/HAPPY GUITAR	Tommy Steele F10976
9	BALLAD OF A TEENAGE QUEEN	Johnny Cash HLS8586
10	ALL I HAVE TO DO IS DREAM/CLAUDETTE	Everly Brothers HLA8618

For popular music, the 1950s was a pivotal period.
At the beginning there was a whole mix of sound – Ted Heath's Band, skiffle, traditional jazz,
crooners like Frank Sinatra, the piano of Winifred Atwell, the voice of Doris Day and Max Bygraves.
Then in 1956 came rock'n'roll with Elvis Presley and Bill Haley's tour of Britain in 1957 – a smash hit.

The Boys' and Girls' Cinema Clubs ANNUAL

ZSA-ZSA GABOR

Picture Sh

SEE INSIDE
(Page 4)

JULIE HARRIS & JAMES DEAN in "East of Eden"

AVA GARDNER AND JAMES MASON

BOB HOPE & MARILYN MAXWELL in The Lemon Drop Kid

THE WORLD'S TOP FILM MAGAZINE

PHOTOPLA

Joan how is her —se

MGM's Lassie

WDL

No 17

6D

THIS IS A WORLD DISTRIBUTORS COMIC

Lassie explores "The Isle of Adventure"

The world seemed full of the most glamorous film stars — Marilyn Monroe, Sabrina, Jayne Mansfield, Diana Dors, Joan Collins, Elizabeth Taylor, Zsa-Zsa Gabor and Brigitte Bardot.

Movies ranged from Hollywood's musical "High Society" (1956) to the epic "Ben Hur" (1959), from the British comedy "The Lavender Hill Mob" (1951) to the classic "Around the World in 80 Days" (1956).

And then there was Lassie — a veteran of the big screen by 1950, Lassie started a new career in 1954 with a television series.

Week ending May 31, 1952   EVERY THURSDAY   3½D

Picturegoer
THE NATIONAL FILM WEEKLY

DEAN MARTIN and JERRY LEWIS

Picture Show &
THE PAPER FOR PEOPLE WHO GO TO THE PICT

TREVOR HOWARD & KERIMA in "Outcast of the Islands"

WE'RE LAUGHING AT THEM NOW   see page 17

EVENTS OF THE 1950s

1950 End of petrol, soap and
paper rationing.
Television's Watch with Mother and
Andy Pandy began.
Eagle comic with Dan Dare
Tide washing powder launched

1951 Festival of Britain
Miss World beauty contest
Winston Churchill became Prime Minister
Girl and TV Comic published
'The Archers' start on radio

1952 King George VI died
Agatha Christie's Mousetrap play op
Sooty on TV. Airfix kits
Surf washing powder launched.

1953 Coronation of Elizabeth II
Mount Everest climbed
End of sweet rationing
What's My Line on television
Topper comic. Daz washing powder

1954 Four minute mile broken by
Roger Bannister
End of all 'wartime' rationing
Frosted Flakes, Sugar Puffs, Wagon Wheels,
Maxwell House instant coffee, Brooke
Bond tea bags, Omo, Tiger comic

1955 Commercial television with
first TV ad for Gibbs SR
Antony Eden became Prime Minister
Guinness Book of Records
Films: On the Waterfront, East of Eden,
The Seven Year Itch

1956 'Suez Crisis', Egypt nationalized
the Suez Canal
Harbenware non-stick saucepans
Squezy washing-up liquid
Corgi toys. Beezer comic

1957 Premium Bonds introduced
Harold Macmillan now Prime Minister
Queen's Christmas message televised
Dixon of Dock Green on TV
Bill Haley toured Britain

1958 CND founded: Aldermaston march
Munich air crash
Eight miles of motorway opened
Stereo records released
Blue Peter programme on BBC TV
Bunty comic, Galaxy chocolate
Picnic bar, Camay toilet soap
Flash and Handy Andy launched

1959 The Mini motor car
Lunik II reached the Moon
Postcodes for Norwich area
Channel crossed by hovercraft
Opal Fruits and Caramac bars